Contents

It Begins with Bagels

Wire baskets filled with bagels wait for customers at Panera Bread®. The popular everything bagel looks like a spice rack spilled all over it.

The everything bagel doesn't have *everything* on it. But it's got the right spices to pack a flavorful punch. Tiny black poppyseeds and browned sesame seeds are only the beginning. This bagel also has toasted onion, dried garlic, and salt.

Panera BREAD®

FAVORITE FOOD FRANCHISES

Laura Purdie Salas

Mitchell Lane
PUBLISHERS

Parent and Caregiver Tips for Creating Nonfiction Readers

The high-interest topics in the ***Favorite Food Franchises*** series are sure to get your young reader excited about reading nonfiction. While exploring a fascinating subject, your reader will be introduced to new facts, ideas, and vocabulary.

Tips for Reading Nonfiction

Talk about Nonfiction

Explain that nonfiction books provide facts about real-world topics. When readers read nonfiction, they gain a rich understanding of the world. They build background knowledge that provides a foundation for learning and academic success.

Look at the Parts

This book contains the following helpful features. Share the purpose of each feature with your reader.

Photos, Captions, and Graphic Aids

The photos, captions, maps, diagrams, time lines, and other graphic aids in nonfiction texts contain a wealth of information. Help your reader identify different ways information can be displayed.

Sidebars

These extra tidbits of information help satisfy readers' curiosity and expand their knowledge.

Table of Contents

Located at the front of the book, this list shows the big ideas within the text and the page numbers where they can be found.

Glossary

Located at the back of the book, the glossary defines key words and phrases that are related to the topic. These words and phrases can be found in the text in colored type.

Comprehension Questions (Fact Check)

Multiple-choice questions help readers self-check to make sure they understand what they read.

Index

Located at the back of the book, the index is an alphabetical list of topics and the page numbers where they can be found.

With a little help and guidance, your reader will be on their way to enjoying and learning from nonfiction books.

Mitchell Lane
PUBLISHERS
mitchelllanepub.com

2001 SW 31st Avenue
Hallandale, FL 33009

First Edition, 2025.
Author: Laura Purdie Salas
Designer: Rhea Magaro
Editor: Kim Thompson

Series: Favorite Food Franchises
Title: Panera Bread / by Laura Purdie Salas

Hallandale, FL : Mitchell Lane Publishers, [2025]

Library bound ISBN: 979-8-89260-312-6
Paperback ISBN: 979-8-89260-436-9
eBook ISBN: 979-8-89260-318-8

PHOTO CREDITS
Alamy: TheWorldAroundUs, 15; ZUMA Press Inc, 17; Michael Bush, 25; Panera Bread: 5, 6, 19, 21, Public Domain: Melanie Landsman/The Luupe, 14; Shutterstock: BWM Infinity, cover, 1; dwph, cover; Deutschlandreform, 3; David P. Smith, 4; rangizzz, 5, 9, 10, 13, 16, 18, 20, 23, 27; ZikG, 7; DCStockPhotography, 9; GreenArt, 11; Khairil Azhar Junos, 12; Nanisimova, 13; DragonTiger8, 15; photobeps, 16; S Becker, 18; Madlen, 20; Dmitry Kovalchuk, 20; Nolichuckyjake, 22; woodsnorthphoto, 22; Triff, 22; jejim, 22; Barre Kelley, 23; JHVEPhoto, 23; Kathy Hutchins, 24; sentretvector, 24; VH-studio, 26; PLotulitStocker, 27; Feng Cheng, 29; Suradech Prapairat, 32; Wikimedia: 8

Knead to Know

The cinnamon crunch bagel is another Panera favorite. It's baked with cinnamon and vanilla chips and has a sweet, crunchy, outer layer. One thing you'll notice right away is what's missing. There's no hole in the middle!

Bagels are not the only option at this successful restaurant chain. The company offers soups, salads, sandwiches, smoothies, breakfast items, and more. Unlike many quick-serve restaurants, Panera has lots of healthy, plant-based choices on the menu.

Panera calls its locations bakery-cafés. You can buy a **baker's dozen** of bagels or a whole loaf of bread like you would at a bakery. You can also sit and eat lunch or enjoy a cup of coffee like you would at a café.

FAMILY FRIENDLY
FLATBREADS.
FLATBREAD PIZZA
FAMILY FEAST
CHOOSE ANY 2 FLATBREAD PIZZAS AND 2 WHOLE SALADS. STARTING AT $24.

The Business of Bread

Ron Shaich is the **founder** of Panera. In 1981, he opened a tiny cookie shop in Boston, Massachusetts. Nobody bought cookies during the morning, so he decided to sell baked goods he got from a small chain of bakeries called Au Bon Pain.

Eventually, the cookie shop and the bakeries merged to create the Au Bon Pain company. Shaich was the **CEO**. Au Bon Pain grew. It opened more locations. In 1985, the restaurant chain began selling soups and sandwiches.

Ron Shaich

Knead to Know

The phrase *au bon pain* is French. It means "from good bread." The name Panera comes from the ancient Latin word *pānārium*. It means "bread basket."

In 1993, Au Bon Pain bought a chain of bakeries in the state of Missouri. It was called the St. Louis Bread Company. It inspired the creation of the first Panera Bread bakery-cafés. In 1999, Shaich sold the Au Bon Pain division to focus on Panera.

Bakers at the St. Louis Bread Company used a **sourdough starter** that originally came from San Francisco, California. Panera says that yeast from that same starter is still used today to make its sourdough bread.

Knead to Know

All of Panera's Missouri locations still carry the name St. Louis Bread Company.

Visiting Panera

Panera customers can order on a digital device or at the counter. Some **franchises** give you a buzzer that vibrates when your order's ready to pick up. At other locations, your food gets delivered to your table.

Panera wants customers to come in and stay awhile. Restaurants have soft, comfortable furniture in warm colors. Fireplaces and wooden tables add to the cozy vibe.

Friends meet for coffee or lunch. Other people come to work. They sit with their laptops, papers, and phones.

Knead to Know

Some Panera locations have ovens out where customers can see them. Bread bakes during the day so people can catch a whiff of deliciousness.

UNLIMITED SIP CLUB
KEEP THE
COFFEE
COMING
UNLIMITED SIP CLUB

Over the years, Panera has provided new experiences for customers. In 2004, the company was the largest free Wi-Fi provider in the United States. In 2010, Panera became the first national restaurant chain that volunteered to include calorie information on its menu.

Kiosks for self-ordering and options for mobile ordering were introduced in 2012. In 2022, the first digital-only Panera To Go location opened near Chicago, Illinois. It has no dining room and is for pick-up orders only.

Take a Taste

Baked goods are the star of the menu at Panera. There are **baguettes**, bagels, and bread bowls. The bakery case is filled with tempting cookies, cinnamon rolls, and chocolate croissants.

These items are not made from scratch at Panera locations. The company has long used Fresh Dough Facilities (FDF). FDF bakers make the dough, knead it, and roll it out. Then, it's delivered to each franchise and baked on site.

Things began changing in the 2020s. Some FDFs closed. Some Panera franchises began using bread that was partially baked and then frozen. This was a big change for a restaurant chain that has prided itself on serving freshly prepared food.

Knead to Know

Panera uses fresh vegetables. But most soups, pastas, and meats arrive at each franchise already cooked and frozen.

BAGELS, CREAM CHEESE & MORE
Orange Scone

There's more on the Panera menu. Customers can choose a variety of breakfast, lunch, and dinner items. A cold day calls for tomato soup or broccoli cheddar soup. Want more vegetables? Grab a Greek salad or a southwest chicken ranch salad. Craving a sandwich? Try tuna salad or bacon avocado.

Panera was one of the first restaurant chains to offer two small **entrées** as a meal. The option is called You Pick Two®. Maybe you'd like mac and cheese with a strawberry poppyseed chicken salad. Good choice!

Knead to Know

A large Charged Lemonade at Panera contained 390 milligrams of caffeine. That's about four times the amount of caffeine in a cup of coffee. Lawsuits about the drink claimed that it led to the deaths of two customers who already had health problems.

Panera promises that it serves only clean food. That means its menu is free of artificial **preservatives**, sweeteners, flavors, and colors. The company also claims that many of its meals are **sustainably** produced using methods that don't advance climate change. These meals include lots of grains, beans, fruits, and vegetables. The idea is to serve food that is tasty, healthy, and good for the planet.

Knead to Know

The Panera No No List includes about 70 chemical additives that are not allowed in its foods. These include colorings, flavorings, high-fructose corn syrup, and artificial trans fats.

THE NO NO LIST

Panera BREAD®

At Panera Bread, "Clean" describes food that does not contain the artificial preservatives, sweeteners, flavors, and colors from artificial sources on this "No No List". You won't find any of these in our ingredient statements for our US bakery-cafe food menu and grocery products.

Acesulfame K (Acesulfame Potassium)

Advantame

Alum (Aluminum Ammonium Sulfate/ Aluminium Potassium Sulfate)

Ammonium Chloride

Artificial Colors (Certified FD&C)

Artificial Flavors

Aspartame

Astaxanthin

Azo Dyes

Azodicarbonamide

Benzoic Acid

Benzyl Alcohol/Benzoyl Peroxide

BHA (Butylated Hydroxyanisole)

BHT (Butylated Hydroxytoluene)

Bromated Flour

Brominated Vegetable Oil

Calcium Bromate

Calcium Peroxide

Canthaxanthin

Caprocaprylobehenin

Caramel Color (Classes II-IV)

Carboxymethyl Cellulose (CMC/ Cellulose Gum)

Carmine/Cochineal

DATEM (Diacetyl Tartaric Acid)

Diacetyl/Acetoin

Disodium Guanylate (GMP)

Disodium Inosinate (IMP)

EDTA (Calcium Disodium EDTA/ Disodium Dihydrogen EDTA)

Esters of Fatty Acids (Glycerol and Polyglycerol Esters)

Ethoxyquin

Fat Substitutes (Sucrose Polyester, Microparticulated Whey Protein Concentrate)

Glycerides (Mono, Di & Triglycerides, all forms)

Glycerol Ester of Wood Rosin

High Fructose Corn Syrup (HFCS)

Hydrogenated Starch

Hydrolyzed Soy or Corn Protein

Lard

L-Cysteine (Cystine)

Monosodium Glutamate/ Sodium Glutamate

Neotame

Nitrates/Nitrites

Parabens (all forms)

Partially Hydrogenated Oils/ Artificial Trans Fat

Polydextrose

Polyethylene Glycol (PEG)

Polysorbates (all forms)

Potassium Benzoate

Potassium Bromate

Potassium Lactate

Propionates (Calcium, Potassium, Sodium)

Propionic Acid

Propyl Gallate

Propylene Glycol

Propylene Glycol Alginate

Saccharin (Calcium Saccharin)

Salatrim

Silicates/Clay minerals (all forms)

Silicones/Siloxanes (Methyl Silicon, Dimethylpolysiloxane)

Sodium Benzoate

Sodium Diacetate

Sodium Erythorbate

Sodium Lactate

Sodium Lauryl Sulfate

Sorbates (Calcium, Potassium, Sodium)

Stannous Chloride

Sucralose

Sucroglycerides

Sulfites (Added, not naturally occurring)

Tertiary Butylhydroquinone (TBHQ)

Theobromine

Titanium Dioxide

Triacetin/Glycerol Triacetate

Ethylvanillin/Vanillin

Last Updated: 1/1/24

Panera and People

More than 2,100 Paneras operate across the United States. Canada has a few franchises too. Over 100,000 people work at the company.

Although people of all ages eat at Panera, customers tend to be older than at many quick-serve restaurant chains. The company has more women customers than men.

Homestead, PA

Charlotte, NC

San Jose, CA

Spring, TX

Ontario, Canada

Knead to Know

Some Panera locations have community rooms that can be reserved for meetings by local clubs and organizations.

Panera relies on word-of-mouth advertising. It hopes that happy customers will tell other people how great it is. It doesn't have a lot of snappy slogans or popular commercials.

The company does use TikTok and celebrities to reach younger customers. Singer and rapper T-Pain helped promote a new sandwich. And singer Michael Bolton made a spoof of his hit version of "When a Man Loves a Woman." The new song was called "When Some Mac Loves Broccoli Cheddar."

Michael Bolton

T-Pain

Panera serves soups, salads, and sandwiches. It also serves communities. The Panera Bread Foundation focuses on supporting children and teens. Some of its programs help kids get ready for college. Others teach job and life skills.

Another charity is Panera's Day-End-Dough-Nation program. Each night, Panera locations donate their unsold baked goods. These donations feed young people, veterans, and other people facing **food insecurity**.

Knead to Know

In the 2010s, Panera operated five franchises with a goal of raising awareness about food insecurity. Customers had to pay only what they were able to. Eventually, all five locations lost too much money and closed down.

A Panera Time Line

1981 Ron Shaich opens the Cookie Jar in Boston. It merges with the Au Bon Pain bakery.

1985 Au Bon Pain adds soups and sandwiches to its menu.

1993 Au Bon Pain buys the St. Louis Bread Company.

1999 Au Bon Pain sells off its Au Bon Pain division to grow its Panera division.

2008 Panera expands into Canada.

2010 Panera is growing so quickly that it opens a new franchise approximately every three days.

2015 Panera issues a No No List of artificial ingredients it does not allow in its recipes.

2016 Panera's 2,000th location opens in Ohio.

2017 Founder Ron Shaich sells Panera to JAB Holding Co. for 7.5 billion dollars.

2021 Panera joins Caribou Coffee and Einstein Bros. Bagels to form Panera Brands.

2022 Panera opens its first digital-only location, Panera To Go.

2024 Highly caffeinated Charged Lemonade drinks are dropped from the menu.

Panera
BREAD

Glossary

baguettes (ba-GETS)
long, skinny loaves of French bread

baker's dozen (BAY-kurz DUHZ-uhn)
thirteen

CEO (see ee oh)
acronym for *chief executive officer*; the top leader of a company

entrées (AHN-trays)
items that are usually main courses of a meal

food insecurity (food in-si-KYOOR-uh-tee)
the situation of not being able to get or afford enough food

founder (FOUN-dur)
the person who starts a company or organization

franchises (fran-CHYE-sis)
individual locations of a chain store or restaurant; legal agreements that let people run businesses that sell products created by a larger company

preservatives (pri-ZUR-vuh-tivz)
chemicals added to food to keep it from spoiling

sourdough starter (SOUR-doh STAR-tur)
a living culture of yeast and bacteria that is used to make bread rise and that is created by combining flour and water and allowing the mixture to ferment over time

sustainably (suh-STAY-nuh-blee)
done in a way that can be continued for a long time and that doesn't use up natural resources